What Our Readers Have Said...

Applicability

"These books are great tools that should be used as guidelines for our everyday supervisory practices. You need to take the time to do a short self-evaluation when reading them."

•

"The Pinpoint Training Series delivers information that could be used in a lot different areas."

•

"The things and problems we deal with everyday are discussed in these books."

Convenience

"I like this because I can take them with me to read at a convenient time. I feel the little time I have to spend in the office is best use on activities that directly relate to revenue opportunities. I like the short amount of time it takes to keep up with these."

•

"I prefer the self-study approach; it fits in with my schedule."

•

"I like the fact that the format allows the books to be reviewed as time permits. All work has been conducted on personal, evening/weekend time."

•

"Easy to use... if you put the time into it."

Challenge

"My thought is that the real value of these books comes into effect when doing the action plans."

•

"I like the fact that the format allows assignments to be reviewed as time permits."

Clarity

"Short and sweet. These books are easy to comprehend."

•

"Easy to use, understand, and reference if needed."

Relevance

"I have enjoyed reading these books. They are relevant to today's work environment and the ongoing change in the way we manage our workforce."

•

"I believe the contents of the Pinpoint series are excellent. It causes one to reflect on the daily dynamics in working with oneself as well as with management and peers."

Maximizing Financial Performance

Pinpoint Leadership Skill Development Training Series

TIMOTHY F. BEDNARZ

MAJORIUM
BUSINESS PRESS

Pinpoint Leadership Skill Development Training Series
"Maximizing Financial Performance"
Timothy F. Bednarz

Graphic design: Monika Pawlak

Majorium Business Press
2025 Main Street
Stevens Point, WI 54481
715.342.1018 • 800.654.4935

ISBN 978-1-882181-77-3

Printed in the United States of America

Introduction

The Pinpoint Leadership Skill Development Training Series is designed for targeted training and education regarding increased improvement in a specific skill or competency.

Each book within this series is designed to be easy to use, understand and apply to your job. It can be used as a basis for training individuals, as a discussion guide or as a personal training tool.

Each chapter within this book discusses a specific concept. When you have completed all eight chapters you should have a 360° perspective of the topic.

Additionally, each chapter is divided into specific sections:

- The first section provides you with an overview of the topic
- The Implications section discusses why the concept is important, and why it is important to learn and apply.
- The Strategies, Tips & Techniques to Apply section teaches how to use and apply the particular concept to your work.
- The Points to Ponder section gives you something to think about or to be discussed with a group setting. These are questions not meant to be immediately answered, but to be pondered over time.
- The Training Activity section provides you with the tools to transfer what you have learned to your job. It is designed to help create an action plan to effectively apply the concept.

Each of the topics in this series is time-tested and proven in the marketplace. They have been used by thousands of employees as training tools. Many of the users have commented that what made these books valuable, was the ability to refer to them when a problem surfaced. They indicated that they remembered reading about the exact problem. They referred back to these books and found an appropriate solution.

You will find them equally valuable as a resource in your professional development library.

Table of Contents

1. What Constitutes Financial Performance....1

2. Why Achieving Maximum Financial Performance Is Essential....5

3. Factors That Impact Financial Performance....11

4. How Leaders Impact Financial Performance....15

5. Performance Measurement Systems....19

6. Maintaining Financial Control Using Performance Management Systems....23

7. Identifying Triggering Events....27

8. Linking Performance Indicators to Decision Making....31

LEARNING OBJECTIVES:

- To identify the critical factors and implications comprising financial performance.
- To understand why achieving maximum levels of financial performance is essential.
- To identify the factors and elements impacting financial performance.
- How leaders personally impact and influence overall organizational financial performance.
- How to effectively identify and apply specific budgets and metrics for financial performance.
- How to successfully maintain control over organizational financial performance.
- To identify and analyze specific triggering events that work to indicate possible financial performance problems.
- To effectively link financial performance to other organizational units.
- To identify and define performance indicators as they relate to decision making.

1

What Constitutes Financial Performance

Financial reports are used as a conventional means for leaders to communicate and reflect the financial condition of the company and the results of its operations. The reason that financial reports are used as a communication tool is that they transmit data and information that is easily understood by both the sender and the receiver. This is effective because financial reporting adheres to standard accounting principles and conventions.

IMPLICATIONS — WHAT THIS MEANS TO YOU

Financial reports and data provide leaders with the tools to interpret their actions and activities in consistent and uniform terms that are understood by everyone within the organization.

It is important for leaders to understand that the use of standard accounting practices and terms ensures that results and performance are both accurately reported and accounted for. Additionally, the use of a common financial language gives individuals within the organization, investors, and shareholders the ability to understand what is happening and why it is occurring. This forms the basis of accurate decision making and feedback.

Since financial reporting puts constraints on management and compels them to produce accurate data, it is an effective means for leaders, investors and stakeholders to measure overall performance. There are a number of factors discussed below that leaders need to understand related to financial reports as measurement tools.

Emphasis on Income

A summary of operating results within an organization exposes actions that have taken place; revenues and expenses represent these actions. Typically a company will produce an income statement that provides this information in detail. A balance sheet accompanies the income statement and lists the company's assets, its liabilities and the stockholders' equity. The two documents are linked together, as the net income reported on an income statement is transferred to the balance sheet.

Expression in Monetary Units

A monetary unit (e.g. the dollar) is used as a common denominator to permit the combination of dissimilar activities into meaningful summaries and the report them in operating statements by product lines, departments, divisions and the company as a whole. Most companies do not have common denominators to report results, although they may also measure production in terms of tonnage or units produced. Additionally, monetary expressions allow companies to summarize their assets and liabilities into other reports and summaries, such as balance sheets.

Emphasis on Net Earnings

While sales and revenues are important indicators of volume and activity, they do not accurately reflect the costs and expenses to produce the products and services of a company.

"The cost of goods sold" is a phrase used to reflect the costs directly associated with producing a specific product or service. These are often reflected on an income statement, but the cost of goods sold does not show the indirect costs that must also be accounted for. These include non-production costs—human resources, distribution, sales and marketing—that companies need in order to sell, market and support the production of their products and services.

When all of these costs and expenses are accounted for and deducted from the gross sales number, the net income, or earnings of a company is produced.

Importance of Comparative Data

Comparative data allows leaders to measure performance across periods of time—for example, current year-to-date performance vs. last year's corresponding period of performance. While this information does not provide insight into future performance, it is a useful method for judging and evaluating current performance and for noting developing company trends. This data focuses leaders on areas that need specific attention to improve performance.

Comparing Performance Against Budgets

Most leaders submit operating budgets at the beginning of the fiscal year as part of the annual planning process. Most of these budgets are broken into monthly or quarterly segments that allow leaders to evaluate their budgeted performance against the actual results they were able to produce. This performance tool allows leaders to take action to adjust to actual conditions and to improve their performance in future quarters.

Consistency in Accounting Practices

Accounting practices must always be consistent in order to produce accurate year-to-year comparisons. If practices are inconsistent then the resulting reports can be inaccurate and misleading. These good accounting practices are only replaced when significantly better practices become available.

POINTS TO PONDER — SOMETHING TO THINK ABOUT

1. How familiar are you with the financial results produced by your organizational unit?
2. Do you understand how to interpret financial results and their meaning to your organizational unit?

TRAINING ACTIVITY — APPLICATION & ACTION PLAN

Examine an operating statement for your department or division.

1. Identify the sales or volume your organizational unit produces.
2. Identify the costs associated with the production of your product or services.
3. Identify the indirect costs associated with your unit.
4. Identify the net profit of your organizational unit.

2

Why Achieving Maximum Financial Performance Is Essential

The necessity for organizations to maximize their financial performance has been heightened and intensified by global competitive forces. The current financial structures of companies based in what were once considered Third World Pacific Rim countries gives many of them dramatic financial advantages over U.S.-based manufacturing companies.

IMPLICATIONS — WHAT THIS MEANS TO YOU

The impact of globalization has been building since the mid-to-late 1960s after most of the world's infrastructure, destroyed during World War II, was rebuilt. Suddenly, the impact of new plants and equipment and more advantageous labor laws placed U.S. companies at a distinct economic disadvantage. Many of these companies were hindered by older equipment and outmoded labor agreements. The flexibility to react to change was not there, and the management structure in place was not accustomed to the global competition threatening their survival.

It is important for leaders to understand that the vast waves of change that have altered the landscape of American business did not develop in a void. Traumatic upheavals in many businesses were directly caused by the globalization of industry, changing the way companies produced and competed. These forces remain unabated, pressuring companies and industries with the need to ensure maximum financial performance.

STRATEGIES, TIPS & TECHNIQUES TO APPLY

An organization's ability to either thrive or simply survive is dependent upon a number of ever-present variables, which are discussed in this section. An understanding of these variables will allow leaders to better comprehend their global competitive position.

Labor

The labor structure of a company is comprised of the employees, their wages and the benefits that each accrues. In many organizations in the United States, union labor contracts represent a high cost for companies to bear. Collective bargaining agreements ensure that union members receive a negotiated hourly wage together with generous benefit packages. These contracts often hinder a company's ability to be flexible in the face of change and to successfully compete globally.

When the typical wage and benefits package for the U.S. worker is compared to that of an Asian counterpart, the U.S. hourly wage often eclipses the foreign worker's weekly pay. This financial situation automatically places many U.S.-based companies at a disadvantage since labor represents a high percentage of their cost structure.

Materials

Material costs can swing in either direction, depending upon the sources of the materials and the transportation costs to get them to a manufacturing facility. The closer the source of materials to the manufacturing facility, the cheaper the costs will be. Thus, depending upon the industry, the material costs associated with producing goods for a global economy can be considered neutral.

Overhead

The overhead costs associated with producing goods and services at a specific geographic facility will vary. Typically foreign competitors, especially on the Pacific Rim, enjoy a large financial advantage over companies with manufacturing facilities in the United States. However, this is one area that is constantly in flux, where leaders can have an impact in reducing costs through greater efficiency and increased productivity. This is true since most overhead costs are proportional to the volume produced in a manufacturing facility.

Two additional factors that impact local overhead costs are:

Laws and Regulations – The cost of implementing environmental, safety and labor laws and regulations at a specific location directly impact the facility's overhead structure. Companies located in the United States have restrictive state and federal laws and mandates that they must comply with that don't exist in many foreign countries. The costs associated with the implementation and compliance with these laws add substantially to the overhead that a company must absorb and pass along to their customers as price increases.

Tax Codes – In addition to the costs of regulations, laws and mandates, the local tax structure places further burden on U.S. companies, which foreign companies are often free from. The cost of social programs, welfare and other expenses that raise taxes appreciably are all paid for by corporations and passed along to consumers, who ultimately pay these penalties through higher product costs and their own taxes. In many situations, the overall tax burden placed upon American companies puts them in an uncompetitive position in relation to their foreign competitors.

Plant and Equipment Replacement

The cost of replacing and updating existing plants and equipment is an important competitive consideration. These costs are impacted by the tax codes that allow companies to depreciate their plant or equipment on a predetermined schedule. Additionally, as companies consider the costs to upgrade or replace plants and equipment, more are looking at other financial factors—

labor costs, materials, overhead, taxes, laws and regulations—as part of their overall decision.

Overall Impact

Taken together, the financial factors listed within this lesson describe the global competitive position a company is placed in. All of these factors must be covered by the price of a product, including a desired profit margin. If the costs of a domestic company are much higher that those of a foreign competitor, the foreign competitor can charge a lower price and still achieve a higher profit margin. The domestic company may need to reduce their profit margin to match the foreign competitor's price. In the long run, reduced profits threaten the survival of the company since these contribute to new investments in research, plants, equipment and jobs. Any competitive advantage slowly erodes with reduced profitability.

POINTS TO PONDER – SOMETHING TO THINK ABOUT

1. How aware have you been about the financial impact of global competition on your company?
2. Have you considered the impact each financial factor has on your company?

TRAINING ACTIVITY – APPLICATION & ACTION PLAN

1. Review your company's competitive position.
2. Compare your company against several major foreign competitors using the following financial factors.
    - Labor

- Materials
- Overhead
    - Laws and Regulations
    - Tax Codes
- Plant and Equipment Replacement

3. Identify where your company has the financial advantage and why.
4. Determine how your company can remain globally competitive.

3

Factors That Impact Financial Performance

Before leaders and managers can understand financial performance, they must appreciate the key factors of success that are the foundation of financial performance in all organizations. Unfortunately, many individuals do not understand this reality. The inability to understand the foundation of the business creates a single focus, or myopia, that can ultimately have long-term negative consequences on the organization.

IMPLICATIONS – WHAT THIS MEANS TO YOU

Financial performance and the factors that affect it are founded upon managerial, organizational and economic theory. Many leaders are unaware of these principles because they have been forgotten or never taught. Additionally, many leaders are focused on daily activities and responsibilities, which prevent them from taking the time to consider the principles that the organization is founded upon and that drive its success.

It is important for leaders to understand that their tactical myopia on daily activities undermines their ability to think in ways that benefit the entire organization. Tactical myopia keeps the focus on their specific responsibilities or segment of the organization. Instead of thinking strategically about issues like serving the customer, they may be focused on producing more units, improving overall quality, or something more immediate to them. While these areas of focus all certainly contribute to overall organizational goals, the individual leader's thinking is shaped into making these issues and concerns the organization's central focus. This hinders their ability to contribute to the organization's success as they become trapped by constraints of their own making.

STRATEGIES, TIPS & TECHNIQUES TO APPLY

There are a number of key business and economic factors that serve as the foundation of any organization and its financial performance. Many of these are not clearly understood by many leaders and managers, yet they serve as the framework upon which all performance is ultimately gauged. These important factors are discussed in this section.

Cost Centers

Many organizations will commonly use the term "profit centers" to describe various components within an organization. In reality, what is really being gauged is a "cost center." There are no profit centers in any organization, only cost centers that consume resources and efforts and incur costs.

Results

The results as gauged by profits are dependent upon someone outside of the organization. In most cases the outside arbitrator is the customer, who alone decides whether or not the efforts of a business produce positive economic results.

Knowledge

Many leaders will make a determination that the resources of a company—its employees, equipment and physical facilities—are what make it distinctive in the marketplace. In reality, the one and only thing that makes an organization distinctive is its knowledge. This distinctiveness is defined by an organization's ability to use its knowledge—scientific, technical, economic, social and managerial—to produce something of value to the marketplace. The value is ultimately determined by the customer and his or her willingness to purchase the product or service, not by the organization. In this regard, a business is defined as a process that converts knowledge into outside results as measured by an economic value.

Opportunity

The economic value produced, or what is defined as business, comes from taking advantage of opportunities, not from solving existing problems. Successful organizations allocate resources to opportunities. Doing things right solves problems, which, in turn, increases efficiency. But results are only produced when the right things to do are discovered and resources and efforts are concentrated in that particular direction.

Profits

Market leadership produces economic results. Profits are rewards, as allocated by customers, for making a unique and meaningful business contribution. Profits can only be earned by providing something the customer accepts as valuable and is willing to pay for. The organization that wants to produce economic results with something of real value to customers has to develop a leadership position in the market. Even if an organization produces a large volume of products and services, without a leadership position the business will be marginalized, incapable of surviving in the long run.

Change

Market leadership positions are short-lived, temporary advantages. What exists today is already becoming old and outdated. It is the responsibility of leaders to constantly evolve and to reactivate the organization's leadership position through change and innovation.

POINTS TO PONDER — SOMETHING TO THINK ABOUT

1. How well have you incorporated these key factors of economic success in your daily thinking and decision making?
2. How often have you considered these issues in both minor and major decisions?

TRAINING ACTIVITY — APPLICATION & ACTION PLAN

Reinforce your organization's key factors of success.

1. Define how your organization converts knowledge into outside results as measured by an economic value.
2. Determine how your organization produces results: find the right things to do and concentrate resources and efforts on them.
3. Define how your organization develops a leadership position in the market: produce something of real value to the customer.

4

How Leaders Impact Financial Performance

Financial performance within an organization is impacted on many levels. Leaders can implement a cost-cutting program, and they can shift business resources in response to new opportunities that might have a strong and positive impact on the organization. Both actions are valid, and both need to be understood by leaders to be effective.

IMPLICATIONS — WHAT THIS MEANS TO YOU

Organizational leadership must extend beyond the leader's own area of responsibility to the organization as a whole to see how it uses its financial resources to attain specific outcomes in distinct result areas. Financial performance is attained when leaders understand the use of organizational resources and implement strategies to ensure that they are used in critical areas that most positively impact the performance of the organization.

It is important for leaders to understand that the proper use and implementation of key business resources is fluid and shifts with the needs and demands placed upon the organization by the forces of change. Often, in response to specific opportunities, leaders must be able to shift available resources to take advantage of them. They must understand what can be shifted and why, and know which resources are not within their control to maximize. While accounting terms and procedures are used to measure these abilities, leaders must understand the foundation of financial performance and how these factors impact the organization.

STRATEGIES, TIPS & TECHNIQUES TO APPLY

Financial performance is impacted by a number of variables. Cost controls at local levels are important. But from an organizational perspective, leaders must understand that measurable financial impact is based upon an understanding of what business resources are and how they are allocated within the organization. Most important is leaders understanding the utilization of these resources to produce the optimal levels of results for the organization.

Key Business Resources

It is easy for leaders to examine the many resources available to an organization, but all have only two key business resources to focus on. First, well-trained people are the most important key business resource available to an organization and are the one resource that should have the greatest impact on the company. The second key resource is the capital, or money available to an organization that results from revenues and profits and from investments by stockholders and other backers.

Key Leadership Questions

Within any organization, leaders must always question what scarce and expensive resources are being used for. The answers to this inquiry always change as organizations evolve along with the market and the needs of the customer. The environment is never static and always needs to be reviewed.

In addition, leaders must review and examine the result areas (product) where key business resources are being deployed and used. Leaders must consider whether these resources are being applied to the most important and promising opportunities available to the organization or to problem areas that produce less financial impact.

Shifted Resources

In order to impact financial performance, leaders should understand that there are only three resources that can be shifted in an organization within a reasonable time frame to take advantage of opportunities and maximize profitability. These include:

- Knowledge/people
- Working capital
- Operating expenses

Misallocation

Leaders should know that the availability of shifted resources is susceptible to management pressures, urgency and drift. For instance, companies can be tempted to shift resources from a profitable operation or facility to an unprofitable one for a limited period of time to buttress performance. The shift may include key staff members as well as technical and managerial employees. While this may appear logical, it is a misallocation of resources, robbing the most profitable operations of needed and scarce resources. In many instances it will also prove to be ineffective, resulting in not just one, but two problem areas.

Capital Resources

Capital resources or expenditures are typically not an area that leaders can impact unless they are part of a team or committee that decides upon their purchase and implementation. Otherwise, once an investment is made, these resources are immovable. However, there are circumstances where a highly industrious facility can be employed to produce a more profitable product. But these decisions tend to be more strategic than tactical.

Analysis

Leaders can make a difference and financial impact by understanding through analysis where business resources are and how they relate to the desired business results. The real opportunity lies in knowing where managerial expenses are invested and shifting them to the key result areas within the organization for the greatest positive impact.

POINTS TO PONDER — SOMETHING TO THINK ABOUT

1. How much thought have you given to asset use and application in your area of responsibility?
2. Do you feel that the assets under your direction are being best utilized by your organization?

TRAINING ACTIVITY — APPLICATION & ACTION PLAN

Evaluate your current situation and analyze how resources are shifted to take advantage of key opportunities.

1. Identify opportunities that promise the best results for your organization.
2. Determine how resources have been shifted from less profitable to the most profitable opportunities.
3. Determine if these shifts are producing the most desirable results in the most profitable areas.

5

Performance Measurement Systems

The use of performance-based budgets and key performance indicators afford leaders and senior management the means and mechanism to link and measure performance against corporate strategies and goals. According to a survey published by the American Institute of Certified Public Accountants, 80% of respondents use performance measurement systems as a way to achieve business results and create shareholder value.

IMPLICATIONS — WHAT THIS MEANS TO YOU

Without understanding how all elements and individuals of an organization are bound together, it is easy for leaders and employees to have a myopic perspective of their contributions. The use of plans, budgets and metrics provide all with a common mechanism and language to bridge their differences and to understand the performance of the organization and its component units. Once understood, leaders can gain perspective on how their organizational unit fits into the overall plan, how all of the elements link together, and how each unit's performance affects the others'.

STRATEGIES, TIPS & TECHNIQUES TO APPLY

The following elements provide leaders with an overview on how corporate strategy, performance-based budgets, key performance indicators, and people within the organization are linked and work together.

Corporate Strategy

Before leaders can understand the role of budgets and metrics within the organization, they must understand that both stem from the overall corporate strategy. Budgets and metrics are measurement components of the corporate strategy. The overall corporate strategy is the direction that senior management has decided to take the organization. These directions are long-term and are adjusted to actual events through the use of the annual plan. The organization's annual budgets are linked to these goals and objectives and help to formulate the plan for the year.

The key is for organizations to have a sound strategy and then translate it into measures that can be tracked. As the world and its events drive change through an organization, a question often arises: Is the strategy still sound and are the leaders measuring the right things within the organization?

The forces of change can cause senior management to react and modify what is otherwise a sound corporate strategy. In many regards, if the strategy is considered to be sound in the face of change, it should remain the same; however, this does not rule out adjusting the tactics and emphasis within the strategy.

Performance-Based Budgets

Performance-based budgets are linked to the organization's annual plan. Each department within the organization develops their portion of the budget and submits it for consideration and inclusion in the annual plan. Senior management reviews the submitted budgets and revises and approves them according to the overall organizational goals for the year.

Annual department budgets are used to analyze the performance of individual departments based upon actual results. These budgets will often include all of the elements of the department, such as units produced, profitability, costs, payroll and expenses. While the use of performance-based budgets is commonplace, they are lagging indicators of performance; in other words, they are reporting on the performance of a department after the fact, typically monthly or quarterly. They don't provide the measurement mechanisms to identify problems and to arm leaders to take corrective or preventative action.

Key Performance Indicators

Key performance indicators fill the void left by performance-based budgets because they provide leaders with indictors, or metrics that measure things—considered important gauges of daily performance—in both financial and non-financial terms. These measurements can include cash on hand, operating income, mean response time to service calls, cycle time, productivity by machine or department and so forth. Key performance indicators should link budgets, measures and initiatives to the corporate strategy. The metrics used should relate to these indicators, and the data collected should be used to re-evaluate strategic priorities.

Whereas budgets are lagging indicators of the organization's performance, key performance indicators are leading indicators. They provide leaders with immediate feedback showing where time and resources need to be positioned and maximized.

Budgets and Metrics as Management Tools

Budgets and especially metrics provide leaders with information that is immediately actionable. They are both management tools that help leaders pinpoint trouble spots. Additionally, they keep leaders and employees focused on key performance areas that monitoring and possible improvement.

Leaders should recognize, however, that these are only indicators. They don't tell leaders what is going on: people do. The indicators simply focus everyone's attention on the discussion.

POINTS TO PONDER — SOMETHING TO THINK ABOUT

1. What standards do you use to evaluate key performance in your organizational unit?
2. Do the metrics you use provide the depth of information you need to perform effectively?

TRAINING ACTIVITY — APPLICATION & ACTION PLAN

Clarify your understanding of performance-based measurement systems.

1. Identify the key performance indicators for your organizational unit.
2. Identify both the financial and non-financial indicators of your unit.
3. Determine what they should measure and why.
4. Identify how each relates to the overall financial performance of the organization.

6

Maintaining Financial Control Using Performance Management Systems

Performance measurement systems are becoming popular tools in many organizational settings that focus closely on key performance indicators as a means of more accurately and effectively maintaining control over financial performance. In many organizational settings these tools are still measuring basic performance data as leaders learn to refine and adapt accurate measurement standards to assist them with maximizing the organization's performance. However, as experience and expertise in use expands, these management tools will prove effective in helping leaders be more productive.

IMPLICATIONS — WHAT THIS MEANS TO YOU

Leaders can use performance measurement systems related to budgets and metrics reactively or proactively depending upon how the system is initially established and maintained. Data reported in budgets and financial reports are lagging indicators that cause leaders to react after the actual events reported have occurred. Performance metrics can be established as either leading or lagging indicators based upon what they actually measure. How the data is received and interpreted is up to the individual leader.

The use of a performance measurement system and its associated power are within the control of the individual leader. Over time, as they understand its use and application, leaders can create forward-looking indicators that provide insights into future performance trends, problems and opportunities. This system will enable leaders to develop strategies to anticipate what's on the horizon and act accordingly. In a rapidly changing environment, the implementation of these tools can provide organizations with a powerful competitive advantage.

STRATEGIES, TIPS & TECHNIQUES TO APPLY

Leaders must use the data collected and reported in budgets and metrics to evaluate whether they are tracking the right measures and assigning each the proper weight in their decision making process. The following elements should be considered when evaluating the proper measurements to make.

Choosing the Right Metrics

Many companies that use performance measurement systems focus on narrowly defined areas such as cash flow, operating income and sales revenue without understanding what the key drivers of their business and how they relate to performance. In essence, the choice of the proper metrics relates back to the corporate strategy. Once leaders understand the corporate strategy and the elements they are responsible for, they should be able to translate that into specific measures that they can track.

It should be noted that industrial organizations that are removed from the marketplace often experience a "bullwhip effect" during economic downturns. In these circumstances, it may make more sense for leaders to track end-customer sales and inventories, rather than figures related to orders and sales, to develop an accurate sense of the trends in product demand and the impact on overall production.

Using the Right Numbers

Leaders need to determine which cost numbers and metrics they are using when making specific decisions. Well-defined metrics are effective decision making tools. The key is to determine what specifically needs to be measured with what measurement standards, and then identify the key trigger points that indicate what action needs to be taken.

Key performance indicators are useful tools. However, if the wrong numbers or costs are being measured, then the information provided could produce a bias that can be more harmful than helpful in making decisions.

How Many Metrics to Use

Harvard Business School developed what is known as the "balanced scorecard" approach to performance measurement systems. It claims to offer a simple method for articulating long-term strategy to the workforce and monitoring the progress of the company toward those goals. Its elements go beyond the financial measures most companies use to gauge performance because financial data typically makes up less than one-third of the data included on most scorecards. But it is a system that is gaining more popularity among companies.

Balanced scorecard define a company's strategy in terms of specific measurable objectives. While the number will differ from company to company, the objectives typically involve four areas of management: financial, customer, internal and innovation. The program recommends using 23 to 25 metrics.

A common way to address the number of metrics a company requires to measure its performance is to determine the key drivers linked back to the corporate strategy. However, many companies can get bogged down on the actual number of metrics to use. The key is to be zealous about the data collected and analyzed. Over time, leaders should be able to determine if the measures they are tracking and the weight each is given are correct.

The one factor that must be emphasized is that the use of performance measurement systems is fluid, not a single, one-time event. As circumstances change and the organization adapts, the specific metrics may change as well.

POINTS TO PONDER — SOMETHING TO THINK ABOUT

1. Are there certain decisions where metrics would be helpful to you?
2. Are you reacting to budgets and metrics that report the results after the fact or as the event is occurring?

TRAINING ACTIVITY — APPLICATION & ACTION PLAN

1. Identify the key decisions that you need to regularly make.
2. Identify the data and information you require to make those decisions.
3. Determine the key metrics that would be helpful in providing information and data in a fast, frequent and meaningful way.

7

Identifying Triggering Events

The effective manipulation and use of the data and information that is available in the average organization can help leaders guide and direct their organizational units in an efficient and productive manner. It is crucial to know what data the leader needs and what that data represents. More importantly, leaders must know at what point actions and activities should be triggered to sustain productivity and prevent problems from occurring.

IMPLICATIONS — WHAT THIS MEANS TO YOU

Most leaders are drowning in information and starving for knowledge. They are overwhelmed with reams of data and information that are difficult to interpret and understand. Consequently, when faced with increasing demands on their time, most leaders accumulate the information provided to them but fail to take action on it. This is why the use of performance-based measurement systems and key performance indicators and metrics are useful to leaders and their employees, especially when used to trigger specific actions and activities.

When properly established, key performance indicators and metrics provide leaders with a snapshot of the performance of the organizational unit. The supportive data is available, but the metrics provide leaders with the specific knowledge they need to effectively operate their unit. Additionally, when metrics are used with pre-established trigger points, the numbers inform leaders when specific actions and activities need to be taken to maintain efficiency and productivity. This increases effectiveness and guides and directs leaders with the knowledge that they need to perform well.

STRATEGIES, TIPS & TECHNIQUES TO APPLY

The use and application of performance measurement systems and their accompanying key performance indicators and metrics provides leaders with specific trigger points that indicate some form of action needs to be taken. They are akin to a red flag or an alarm that lets leaders know something is outside the normal parameters. The use of metrics and trigger points are helpful because they allow leaders to actively monitor key activities and automatically trigger action without needing to pay close attention to each metric.

The Use of Metrics

The use of metrics allows leaders to maintain an active pulse on the activities of their organizational unit without having to wade through layers of key performance data. The data tracked can include units produced, units sold, average sales price, percentage of waste and so forth. The actual metric is determined by what is deemed an important measurement of the performance of the unit. If a metric is triggered or the individual leader needs to examine some aspect of the metric, he or she can refer to the accompanying data to gain insight and examine specific aspects of the number reported.

Identifying Trigger Points

When leaders establish metrics as key performance indicators, specific trigger points should be predetermined. These triggers should indicate when numbers are outside the prescribed parameters. Leaders then know that some form of action is required on their part.

It is important that leaders decide at which specific points activities need to be triggered. These trigger points should be determined by how much warning leaders feel they need in order to take appropriate corrective action. If remedial action can be immediately taken, trigger points can be set higher;

if remedial actions are anticipated to take longer, trigger points should be set lower. Leaders will find that these points remain fluid until actual conditions dictate optimal settings.

Setting Parameters

Actual working parameters should be the optimal operational ranges that leaders feel their organizational unit should be working within. The range should establish an optimal operational level and an acceptable deviation (e.g. +/- 10%). Once the parameter is exceeded on either the upper or lower end of the range, a trigger point is activated that informs the leader. Leaders need to discuss optimum parameters and acceptable levels of deviation with the members of their unit. Again, unless already firmly established, leaders should allow these levels to remain fluid until actual conditions determine what is realistic and obtainable.

Determining Actions

Once trigger points have been established, leaders should also decide what specific actions would be triggered when the metrics indicate that performance is outside the acceptable range. Actions will vary depending upon whether the higher or lower trigger points are activated. Leaders and the members of their unit will need to determine what each trigger point means and what should be done when activated.

When trigger points are predetermined with specific assigned actions and activities, employees in an empowered workplace who are informed know what to do without the direction of the leader. This allows organizations to increase their response times and to automatically maintain productivity and efficiency.

POINTS TO PONDER — SOMETHING TO THINK ABOUT

1. How actively do you use and monitor your key performance indicators or metrics?
2. How effective have metrics been in helping you lead your organizational unit?

TRAINING ACTIVITY — APPLICATION & ACTION PLAN

1. If you already use metrics and key performance indicators, review them for the elements below.
2. If you do not have metrics and key performance indicators, implement them using these elements.
    - Identifying trigger points
    - Setting parameters
    - Determining actions

8

Linking Performance Indicators to Decision Making

Key performance indicators or metrics allow organizations to create a common reporting system and language that leaders on all levels can understand and use in their decision making. However, performance measurement decisions deliver key information and data that triggers specific decisions and actions at different levels of the organization.

IMPLICATIONS — WHAT THIS MEANS TO YOU

Performance-based measurement systems provide feedback and insight into all levels of leadership within the organization. Local leaders make decisions based upon trigger points and triggered events as well as overall performance of their organizational units. On the other hand, senior managers must take a strategic perspective that links the performance of all organizational units into feedback related to the entire organization's performance; their decisions are global and focus on the sustainability of the entire organization.

It is important for leaders on all levels to understand the links between local performance and the entire organization. Key performance indicators and metrics trigger decisions on multiple levels. Lower trigger points may cause lower levels to react and make decisions and changes based upon the organizational unit in a specific location. Senior leadership will have trigger points at higher levels that concern the performance of the entire organization, compelling them to make decisions and changes based upon the feedback they receive. While the perspectives may be different at various levels of leadership, the use of key performance indicators and metrics allows all leaders to make the decisions that are their responsibility.

STRATEGIES, TIPS & TECHNIQUES TO APPLY

Decisions can be tactical on a local operational level and strategic at a higher leadership level. The decisions are linked in that the strategic decisions will impact tactical decisions, but tactical may not affect strategic. Strategic decisions typically provide leaders with the boundaries and parameters that they must work within. Leaders at all levels must understand that all decisions impact the organization. Daily decisions may not appear to be connected to the major areas discussed in this section, but, ultimately, all decisions made are based in one of these key areas.

Quality of Execution of Organizational Strategies

The availability of performance measurement systems and key performance indicators provides leaders on all levels of the organization with the decision making tools to measure the quality of the strategy that drives the organization. Financial indicators are lagging indicators, while non-financial indicators provide leaders with a balanced view of what is happening. Metrics provide leaders with specific questions to facilitate the organization's ability to make tough decisions and quickly seize opportunities as well as to evaluate how well it adapts to changing technologies and markets.

Improvement of Non-Financial Performance

Non-financial metrics linked with more traditional financial ones provide leaders with the information to make timely decisions that impact their unit's performance and the entire organization's ability to adapt. Triggered events and predetermined trigger points provide pivotal moments for leaders to make key performance decisions. These events can be established on both strategic and tactical levels with individual leaders responsible for making specific decisions within the organization.

Value Creation

More companies are using value creation indexes that focus on the relationship between non-financial performance and the organization's market value. The establishment of a value creation index provides leaders with key insights by establishing direct links between the two areas of focus. Research has shown that a reliance on non-financial performance leads to more accurate forecasts and valuation. Typically the value creation drivers are:

- Innovation
- Quality
- Customers
- Management
- Alliances
- Technology
- Brand
- Employees
- Environment

While value creation is defined and utilized by senior leadership within the organization, its metrics that measure non-financial performance are driven into the organization and become part of the suite of performance measurement tools used by leaders on all levels. Research has shown that intangible elements such as innovation, alliance, management and employees are the key players in producing the organization's value. Within the durable and non-durable manufacturing environment, improvement in key value drivers results in higher market values. These are the indicators that allow organizations to measure and predict future performance.

Efficient Resource Allocation

The balanced use of performance measurement systems that evaluate both financial and non-financial performance metrics allow leaders to efficiently allocate the use of scarce resources throughout the organization. Decisions that effectively manage resource allocation allow organizations to sustain their performance and profitability. While local leadership on the tactical level makes decisions on the use and application of resources, senior leadership on the strategic level is able to ensure that resources are used in ways that benefit the entire organization. The use of performance measurement metrics allows leaders on all levels to evaluate effectiveness and make decisions regarding future performance.

POINTS TO PONDER — SOMETHING TO THINK ABOUT

1. How clearly do you understand the links between your performance and the organization's performance?
2. Do you understand how your performance and the performance of your organizational unit contribute to the success of the entire organization?

TRAINING ACTIVITY — APPLICATION & ACTION PLAN

List on a sheet of paper the key decisions and trigger points that you are specifically responsible for.

1. Identify which decisions are made on a tactical or local level and which are made on a strategic level.
2. Determine the links between your decisions and those made at higher levels of leadership.
3. Identify how decisions made at the strategic level of leadership determine the boundaries and parameters you must work within.

About the Author

Timothy F. Bednarz, Ph.D. is CEO of the American Management Development Group, Inc. For over 20 years he has researched, designed and authored hundreds of learning and development programs used by Fortune 1000 companies.

He is also the author of *Great! What Makes Leaders Great. What They Did, How They Did It and What You Can Learn from It* (2011).

Speaking Availability

Timothy F. Bednarz, Ph.D. is available for speaking engagements for your next meeting or association event. He can be contacted at 800-654-4935 or by e-mail at timothy.bednarz@majorium.com.

Bulk Sales

Bulk sales of this book or any other titles available from Majorium Business Press. Inquiries can be directed to sales@majorium.com, or by phone at 800-6654-4935.

Quick Order Form

Fax orders: 715-342-1118. Send this form.

Telephone orders: Call 800-654-4935 toll-free. Have your credit card ready.

Email orders: sales@majorium.com

Postal orders: Majorium Business Press, 2025 Main Street, Stevens Point, WI 54481, USA.

Please send the following books:

____

____

____

____

Please send more FREE information on:

❑Catalog ❑Speaking/Seminars ❑Mailing Lists ❑Consulting

Name: ____________________________________

Address: __________________________________

City: ____________________ State: _____ Zip: __________

Telephone: ________________________________

Email address: _____________________________

Sales tax: Please add 5.5% for products shipped to Wisconsin addresses.

Shipping by air:

United States: $4.00 for first book and $2.00 for each additional product.

International: $9.00 for first book; $5.00 for each additional product (estimate).

Made in United States
Cleveland, OH
05 November 2026

47675532R00026